Basics of Economics, Grade 3

Table of Contents

W9-BEP-699

Introduction 1

Vocabulary List 2

Assessments
Overall Pretest 3
Overall Posttest 5
Vocabulary Pretest 7
Vocabulary Posttest 9
Applications Pretest 11
Applications Posttest 12

Unit 1: Vocabulary
What Is Economics? 13
Natural Resources 14
Human Resources 15
Capital Resources 16
Conservation of Resources. . . 17

Goods and Services 18
Mario's Business 19

In the Market. 20
Production 21
Producers and Consumers . . . 22
Division of Labor 23
Price 24
Opportunity Cost 25
Chu's Shoes 26

Making a Budget 27
Income and Expenses 28
Taxes and Fees. 29
Public Goods and Services. . . 30
Savings 31
Barter 32
Nick's Budget 33

Unit 2: Applications
What Kind of Resource? 34
Goods or Resources? 35
From Trees to Boards 36
A Shopping Trip 37
A Business Plan. 38
Shirt Production. 39
Let's Build a Playhouse 40
Snack Consumer 41
Which To Buy? 42
A Gift for Yourself. 43
Our Taxes Pay for Services . . 44
Saving Your Money 45
Let's Make a Deal! 46

Answer Key 47

Simplify the Teaching of ECONOMICS

Economics, in its most basic sense, is the study of how people use and transfer resources. We, as well as our students, are familiar with the concepts because they are an intrinsic part of life. Students know that people work and that they need money to buy things. As teachers, when we think of economics, we may recall the study of economic systems and the role of government in the economy. For elementary students, we ask, "Why are we teaching economics?"

• Economics terms and concepts are now included in the elementary curriculum and on state tests.

• Standards and approaches for teaching economics, such as those provided by the National Council on Economic Education, are becoming more evident.

• Students now think more globally.

We also ask, "How can we teach economics?"

• "The man who can make hard things easy is the educator." (Ralph Waldo Emerson)

• *Basics of Economics* is a tool to help you make things easy, to simplify the complex study of economics.

• *Economics doesn't have to be taxing. We only need the form!*

The Form
The nautilus shell can be representative of learning economics. We build a core of language and labels for the concepts from the inside. The learning is spiraled, repeating and incorporating each new term through more complex applications and vocabulary.
• At the core of the nautilus shell is the "golden rectangle."

• The "golden rectangle" has been identified to be the most pleasing shape visually to most humans.

• A credit card has the exact proportional dimensions of the "golden rectangle."

We have used this shell symbol on the pages with vocabulary, the core of economics, so that students can connect labels to familiar concepts in their world. (You may want to learn more about the *golden rectangle*, based on the *Fibonacci sequence*. Either phrase can be used as a search item on the Web.)

Organization and Use of *Basics of Economics*
• **Vocabulary List:** List of terms presented in the order that will help to develop concepts. This order mirrors the presentation in the book.

• **Assessments:** Pretests and posttests to identify needs and mastery.

• **Vocabulary:** Terms are divided into three sections.

   • 7 or 8 vocabulary words in each section

   • pages to introduce the vocabulary words

   • page to incorporate and apply the vocabulary words

• **Applications:** Review, comparison, and use of the vocabulary in entertaining, thought-provoking situations, appropriate for the grade level. Some applications may require a separate piece of paper.

   • Coupon for Extra Credit, the extension activity, is included with many applications.

Note
The newspaper can be a handy aid for teaching economics. Students will benefit from examining advertisements that include the descriptions and prices of goods and services.

*The interest earned on this investment of time is increased **vocabulary** that can be reinvested in daily **applications**.*

Basics of Economics, Grade 3

Vocabulary List

- **Economics**, in its most basic sense, is the study of how people use and transfer resources. There are three general kinds of resources: natural resources, human resources, and capital resources.

- **Natural resources** are things that occur naturally, without human intervention. Examples include water, land, trees, plants, animals, oil, coal, and so forth. Natural resources, sometimes called raw materials, are used to produce goods.

- **Human resources** are the workers themselves. They may be goods workers (who produce a good) or service workers (who perform a service).

- **Capital resources** are the buildings, tools, and equipment used by the workers to produce a good or service.

- **Conservation of resources** means to manage and use our resources wisely.

- **Goods** are things that are produced. Goods range from paper clips to giant airplanes. Capital resources are usually goods, too.

- **Services** are jobs in which people help other people. Teachers, doctors, clerks, barbers, plumbers, maids, and tour guides are all service workers.

- All the resources come together in **production**. Using capital resources (tools and equipment, etc.), human resources (workers) produce a good (using natural resources) or a service.

- Those involved in production are called **producers**. Producers make and sell goods. They also provide services.

- **Consumers** are the people who buy goods and services. Often, consumers have a range of choices, and they may use the price of a good or service as an important consideration in deciding which choice to make. Producers are often consumers, too. Producers must buy goods or services in order to produce their own good or service.

- Often, the various parts of the production process are done by different companies or workers. This splitting up of the various jobs in production is called **division of labor**, or specialization. Consider an assembly line. Each worker on the assembly line performs a different task to produce a finished product.

- **Price** is the amount the consumer pays for a good or service.

- **Opportunity cost** is what a person loses by choosing one opportunity instead of another.

- A **budget** is a plan that shows how much a person earns and spends. A good budget will be balanced, with at least an equal amount of income and expenses.

- **Income** is the money a person makes by working. Specifically, this is called **earned** income. A person can also have **unearned** income from savings accounts, stocks and bonds, or rental properties.

- An **expense** is the money people must spend for a good or service. Most people have several expenses, such as house or apartment payments, gasoline expenses, food and clothing expenses, insurance expenses, health expenses, entertainment expenses, and so forth.

- Most people must also pay **taxes** and **fees**. Taxes are money that the government collects to pay for goods and services it provides to citizens. Fees are extra charges for goods or services that the government provides for the people.

- Tax money usually pays for police and fire departments, public education, postal service, libraries, roads and bridges, social services, national defense, and a variety of other programs. These programs provided by governments are known as **public goods and services**.

- If people have money left over after paying their expenses, they may decide to put that money into a **savings** account. A savings account accumulates unearned income known as interest. People may save money to make a large purchase in the future, such as a house or car, or to pay for college. People may also use their savings for unexpected expenses, such as medical bills or house repairs.

- On occasion, people are able to get goods or services without using money. They trade goods or services for other goods or services. This is called **barter**. Barter works only if both parties in the trade believe that they are getting a fair trade or a good deal.

Overall Pretest

Directions Darken the circle by the answer that best completes the statement.

1. People buy things using
   _____.
   - Ⓐ wood
   - Ⓑ money
   - Ⓒ jokes
   - Ⓓ bites

2. The money a person earns by working is _____.
   - Ⓐ expense
   - Ⓑ inputs
   - Ⓒ income
   - Ⓓ interest

3. The money a person spends to buy something is an _____.
   - Ⓐ expense
   - Ⓑ inputs
   - Ⓒ income
   - Ⓓ exit

4. The cost of a thing is its
   _____.
   - Ⓐ income
   - Ⓑ price
   - Ⓒ tax
   - Ⓓ opportunity

5. Water is a _____ resource.
   - Ⓐ natural
   - Ⓑ human
   - Ⓒ capital
   - Ⓓ conservation

6. A teacher is a _____ resource.

   - Ⓐ natural
   - Ⓑ human
   - Ⓒ capital
   - Ⓓ conservation

7. Money a government collects is a _____.
   - Ⓐ good
   - Ⓑ service
   - Ⓒ tax
   - Ⓓ barter

8. The money a person puts away to use later is called
   _____.
   - Ⓐ taxes
   - Ⓑ expenses
   - Ⓒ savings
   - Ⓓ fees

GO ON ⇨

Overall Pretest, page 2

Directions Write complete sentences to answer the questions.

9. You need a new baseball. Jordan's Sports Store sells baseballs for $5.00 each. The Sports Mart has the same baseballs on sale for $4.00 each. Which would you choose to buy? Tell why.

_____

_____

_____

_____

10. You want to buy a new book that costs $10.00. But you have only $5.00. Tell how you could earn the extra money you need. Name at least three ways.

_____

_____

_____

_____

Overall Posttest

Directions Darken the circle by the answer that best completes the statement.

1. Economics is the study of the use of _____.
   - Ⓐ resources
   - Ⓑ rivers
   - Ⓒ names
   - Ⓓ comets

2. Natural resources are sometimes called _____.
   - Ⓐ tools
   - Ⓑ services
   - Ⓒ raw materials
   - Ⓓ workers

3. A truck driver is a _____ resource.
   - Ⓐ natural
   - Ⓑ human
   - Ⓒ capital
   - Ⓓ conservation

4. _____ sell goods and services.
   - Ⓐ Consumers
   - Ⓑ Producers
   - Ⓒ Taxes
   - Ⓓ Resources

5. _____ buy goods and services.
   - Ⓐ Consumers
   - Ⓑ Producers
   - Ⓒ Resources
   - Ⓓ Expenses

6. A plan showing how much you earn and spend is a _____.
   - Ⓐ budget
   - Ⓑ barter
   - Ⓒ market
   - Ⓓ business

7. A trade that does not use money is called _____.
   - Ⓐ income
   - Ⓑ expense
   - Ⓒ barter
   - Ⓓ budget

8. Governments collect taxes and fees to pay for community _____.
   - Ⓐ income
   - Ⓑ services
   - Ⓒ air
   - Ⓓ savings

GO ON ⇨

Overall Posttest, page 2

Directions Write complete sentences to answer the questions.

9. You want a hamster. You may get one, but you must help pay to take care of it. What expenses would you have to pay for your hamster? Think of at least three expenses.

_____

_____

_____

_____

_____

10. Jason has four old pens he wants to trade. Latoya has a new backpack. Should Latoya trade her new backpack for Jason's old pens? Is this a fair trade? Tell why or why not.

_____

_____

_____

_____

_____

Vocabulary Pretest

Directions Darken the circle by the answer that best completes the statement.

1. People use _____ to buy things.
   - Ⓐ cats
   - Ⓑ money
   - Ⓒ services
   - Ⓓ paper

2. Trees are a _____ resource.
   - Ⓐ natural
   - Ⓑ human
   - Ⓒ capital
   - Ⓓ barter

3. A worker is a _____ resource.
   - Ⓐ natural
   - Ⓑ human
   - Ⓒ capital
   - Ⓓ free

4. A worker does a job to earn an _____.
   - Ⓐ expense
   - Ⓑ income
   - Ⓒ exit
   - Ⓓ ocean

5. A factory is a _____ resource.
   - Ⓐ natural
   - Ⓑ human
   - Ⓒ capital
   - Ⓓ broken

6. Teaching is a _____.
   - Ⓐ service
   - Ⓑ good
   - Ⓒ budget
   - Ⓓ tax

7. Chairs are a kind of _____.
   - Ⓐ good
   - Ⓑ bad
   - Ⓒ service
   - Ⓓ tax

8. You can buy things in a grocery _____.
   - Ⓐ tree
   - Ⓑ market
   - Ⓒ bag
   - Ⓓ lake

GO ON ⇨

Vocabulary Pretest, page 2

Directions Darken the circle by the answer that best completes the statement.

9. _____ is the making of a thing.
   - Ⓐ Goods
   - Ⓑ Income
   - Ⓒ Production
   - Ⓓ Expense

10. Producers sell goods and _____.
    - Ⓐ taxes
    - Ⓑ services
    - Ⓒ workers
    - Ⓓ fees

11. Consumers _____ goods and services.
    - Ⓐ buy
    - Ⓑ sell
    - Ⓒ make
    - Ⓓ forget

12. The _____ of a thing is how much it costs.
    - Ⓐ service
    - Ⓑ price
    - Ⓒ tax
    - Ⓓ budget

13. A budget shows how much you earn and _____.
    - Ⓐ spend
    - Ⓑ find
    - Ⓒ lose
    - Ⓓ burn

14. _____ are the costs of things you must buy.
    - Ⓐ Incomes
    - Ⓑ Expenses
    - Ⓒ Budgets
    - Ⓓ Libraries

15. People pay _____ to the government.
    - Ⓐ barter
    - Ⓑ consumers
    - Ⓒ taxes
    - Ⓓ budgets

16. People can put their extra money in a _____ account.
    - Ⓐ savings
    - Ⓑ losing
    - Ⓒ price
    - Ⓓ opportunity

STOP

Vocabulary Posttest

Directions Darken the circle by the answer that best completes the statement.

1. _____ is the study of how people use resources.
   - Ⓐ Energy
   - Ⓑ Barter
   - Ⓒ Economics
   - Ⓓ Farming

2. Natural resources include _____.
   - Ⓐ climate and communities
   - Ⓑ forests and lakes
   - Ⓒ businesses and stores
   - Ⓓ schools and libraries

3. A doctor is a _____ resource.
   - Ⓐ natural
   - Ⓑ human
   - Ⓒ capital
   - Ⓓ free

4. A copy machine is a _____ resource.
   - Ⓐ natural
   - Ⓑ human
   - Ⓒ capital
   - Ⓓ conservation

5. The products of production are called _____.
   - Ⓐ inputs
   - Ⓑ outputs
   - Ⓒ taxes
   - Ⓓ opportunity costs

6. The resources used in production are _____.
   - Ⓐ inputs
   - Ⓑ outputs
   - Ⓒ taxes
   - Ⓓ fees

7. Giving everyone a different job is called _____.
   - Ⓐ barter
   - Ⓑ saving money
   - Ⓒ division of labor
   - Ⓓ being lazy

8. A budget shows how much you _____ and spend.
   - Ⓐ earn
   - Ⓑ lose
   - Ⓒ find
   - Ⓓ care

Vocabulary Posttest, page 2

Directions Darken the circle by the answer that best completes the statement.

9. A thing's _____ may make its price higher.
   - Ⓐ scarcity
   - Ⓑ scars
   - Ⓒ damage
   - Ⓓ opportunity

10. The price of a thing depends on supply and _____.
    - Ⓐ demand
    - Ⓑ delay
    - Ⓒ trade
    - Ⓓ dentists

11. People earn an _____ by working.
    - Ⓐ income
    - Ⓑ expense
    - Ⓒ opportunity
    - Ⓓ budget

12. A government's expenses are paid with _____.
    - Ⓐ smiles
    - Ⓑ tacks
    - Ⓒ taxes
    - Ⓓ rocks

13. _____ can be used for sudden expenses.
    - Ⓐ Savings
    - Ⓑ Shavings
    - Ⓒ Scarcity
    - Ⓓ Sugar

14. A trade that does not use _____ is called barter.
    - Ⓐ sense
    - Ⓑ money
    - Ⓒ words
    - Ⓓ scissors

15. Producers sell _____ and services.
    - Ⓐ workers
    - Ⓑ taxes
    - Ⓒ goods
    - Ⓓ fees

16. A consumer _____.
    - Ⓐ is the owner of a farm
    - Ⓑ makes costumes in a factory
    - Ⓒ buys goods
    - Ⓓ sells fresh vegetables

STOP

Applications Pretest

Directions Welcome to the Shop and Buy Market. You are a consumer. What goods and services will you choose to buy? Tell why. How much do you think each purchase will cost?

_____

_____

_____

_____

_____

_____

_____

_____

Applications Posttest

Directions Choose your favorite recipe. Write the list of ingredients. Tell what resources are used. Put each kind of resource in the correct column. Your food is a good. Tell what your food is.

Recipe Ingredients:

_____

_____

_____

_____

_____

Resources:

Human	Natural	Capital
_____	_____	_____
_____	_____	_____
_____	_____	_____
_____	_____	_____

Good:

_____

What Is Economics?

Economics is the study of how people use resources. There are three kinds of resources studied in economics. One kind is natural resources, or things that occur in nature. Another kind is human resources, or the people who work. A third kind is capital resources, or the tools and equipment that workers use. Because resources are limited, people must learn to conserve resources.

Money is also an important part of economics. People earn money by working at jobs. They spend the money they earn to buy things. They buy goods and services that they want or need.

Directions Write complete sentences to answer the questions.

1. Do you like to shop? What things do you like to buy?

_____

_____

_____

2. How do you get your money? Do you earn it by doing chores? Do you get money as a gift?

_____

_____

_____

3. What chores do you do at home?

_____

_____

_____

Name _____   Date _____

Natural Resources

Economics is about the use of resources. **Natural resources** are one kind of resource. Natural resources are things that occur in nature. Land, water, and rocks are some natural resources. So are oil, iron, and coal. Plants and animals are natural resources, too. Buildings, streets, and cars are not natural resources.

People do not make natural resources. But people use natural resources to make things. Many things can be made from natural resources. Sometimes, natural resources are called raw materials. From these raw materials, people make finished products.

Directions Draw a circle around the things that are natural resources. Draw a square around the things that are not natural resources.

Human Resources

Human resources are another kind of resource. Human resources are the people who work in jobs. These workers do labor. People have many kinds of jobs. They may make things. They may help other people. People earn money by working. What kind of job do you want when you grow up?

Your teacher is a human resource. A fire fighter is a human resource, too. So are clerks, cowboys, and carpenters. Anyone who works is a human resource. But a machine is not a human resource.

Directions Use words from the box to complete the crossword puzzle.

cook	money	clerk	teacher	farmer	driver	actor

Clues

Across
1. Someone who prepares food
2. Someone who works in a school
3. Someone who operates a bus

Down
1. Someone who works in a store
4. Someone who grows crops
5. Someone who stars in a movie
6. What people earn by working

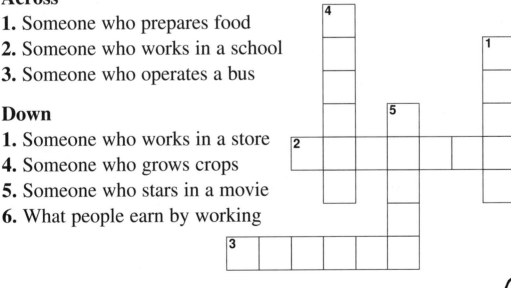

Name _____   Date _____

Capital Resources

   Capital resources are a third kind of resource. Capital resources are made by people. They are used by people to make other things. They may also be used to do work.

   Farmers use tractors to plow their land to grow crops. Workers in factories use machines to make shoes. Plumbers use special tools to fix broken pipes. Tractors, machines, and tools are capital resources. The factory building is a capital resource, too.

Directions Look around your school. What capital resources does your teacher use? Name six things that your teacher uses to help you to learn.

_____

_____

_____

_____

_____

_____

_____

Name _____   Date _____

Conservation of Resources

    We have a limited supply of resources. Many natural resources, such as oil and water, cannot be replaced if they are used up. Forests take a long time to regrow. Soil can become eroded or lose important nutrients.

    Our natural resources should not be wasted or destroyed. We must always work to conserve resources. **Conservation of resources** means to manage and use our resources wisely. Laws have been passed so that people do not waste our precious resources.

    Many things are made from natural resources. If natural resources are wasted, not as many things can be made. Then, the price of those things goes up. If we do not conserve resources, we will have to pay more for the things we buy.

    The average American uses many products made from trees. Each American needs about seven trees a year for those products. How many trees have you used in your lifetime? How can you conserve trees?

Directions Write complete sentences to answer the questions.

1. What are some resources we should conserve, or use wisely?

    _____

    _____

2. What are some ways you can use resources wisely?

    _____

    _____

    _____

Goods and Services

Goods are things that people make or grow. There are many kinds of goods. Pencils, pens, and books are goods. Food and drinks are goods. So are houses, cars, bikes, and gasoline. Some goods are capital resources.

Services are jobs that people do to help other people. People who have service jobs do not make things. Instead, they work to help other people. A teacher does a service by helping students to learn. A doctor does a service by helping people to get well. People who fix broken cars do a service, too. They help people to get their cars running again.

People who have service jobs are called service workers. People who make or grow things are not service workers. They are called goods workers.

People earn money by working. People spend money to buy goods and services. We must have some goods and services to live. These goods and services are called needs. We <u>need</u> food, clothes, shelter, and health care. We like to get other goods and services, but we do not need them. These are called wants. We <u>want</u> a new toy or video game.

Directions The chart shows jobs done by workers. Put an **X** under the word *Goods* if the worker gives us goods. Put an **X** under the word *Services* if the worker gives us services.

Worker	Goods	Services
Judge		
Baker		
Dentist		
Police Officer		
Farmer		

Mario's Business

Mario owns a business. He operates a lawn care service. Michael and Teeka work for Mario. They help him to mow grass and trim trees. They plant bushes and flowers to make the lawns look pretty.

Mario must buy gasoline to run his mowers. Sometimes, he must buy a new mower. He buys saws to cut the tree limbs. He must buy the plants he needs. He must buy shovels and other tools. Sometimes, he buys dirt or rocks for landscaping.

Directions Write complete sentences to answer the questions.

1. What is Mario's service? _____

_____

2. What goods does Mario use? _____

_____

3. What human resources does Mario use? _____

_____

4. What capital resources does Mario use? _____

_____

5. What natural resources does Mario use? _____

_____

Name _____ Date _____

In the Market

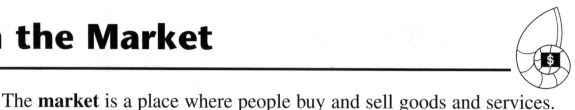

The **market** is a place where people buy and sell goods and services. There are many kinds of markets. You can buy food at a grocery market. You can sell used goods at a "flea market." You can buy shares of a company in the stock market.

In any market, there must be sellers and buyers. Sellers are also known as producers. They use resources to produce goods or services. Then, they sell their goods or services to buyers. Buyers are also known as consumers. They need or want goods and services. They are willing to pay for what they need or want.

Consumers have many choices in the market. They have many opportunities. Sometimes, though, their choice means they get one thing but lose another. This loss is called their opportunity cost.

Directions Three friends are planning the Get-It-Done Helper Company. Write a list of the services they will do. Then, get another piece of paper. Draw the goods they will need to do the services.

_____

_____

_____

_____

_____

_____

_____

www.svschoolsupply.com

© Steck-Vaughn Company

Unit 1: Vocabulary

Economics: Grade 3, SV 3403-7

Production

Production is the way that goods or services are made. Production makes use of the three resources. Human resources are the workers. They use natural resources to produce a good or service. Capital resources are the tools or equipment. The workers need these things to do their job. In production, goods or services are produced.

The resources used in production are known as inputs. Goods and services are the products. These products are known as outputs.

If you go to a restaurant, you can order a meal. A meal is a product. But it must be prepared. Let's say you order some soup. The cook must cut up the vegetables. Next, the vegetables must be cooked. When the soup is ready, it is put in a bowl. Then, a waiter delivers the soup to you. Both goods and services are needed to produce your bowl of soup.

Directions Darken the circle by the answer that correctly completes each statement.

1. Production makes use of the three _____.
   Ⓐ tools
   Ⓑ resources
   Ⓒ workers
   Ⓓ services

2. Capital resources are the _____ the workers need.
   Ⓐ tools
   Ⓑ snacks
   Ⓒ laws
   Ⓓ jobs

3. The resources used in production are called _____.
   Ⓐ consumers
   Ⓑ inputs
   Ⓒ outputs
   Ⓓ producers

4. The products made in production are called _____.
   Ⓐ workers
   Ⓑ inputs
   Ⓒ outputs
   Ⓓ cooks

Price

Price is how much a consumer must pay for a good or service. The same kind of good or service may have different prices. One store may sell a backpack for $12.00. At another store, a similar backpack may cost $10.00. The consumer must decide which is the better choice.

Sometimes the price of a good or service is based on scarcity. Scarcity means that not enough goods or services are available. A producer does not have enough of a thing to supply its consumers. Then, the price of the thing goes up. People will pay more to get the goods or services they want. This system is known as supply and demand.

Scarcity exists because there are not enough resources to produce all the things that people want. For example, the supply of a natural resource such as oil might be low. Then, the price of oil goes up. If we do not conserve our natural resources, prices will only go higher.

Directions You get $3.00 to spend on school supplies. What will you choose to buy? Circle the things in the box you can buy for your $3.00.

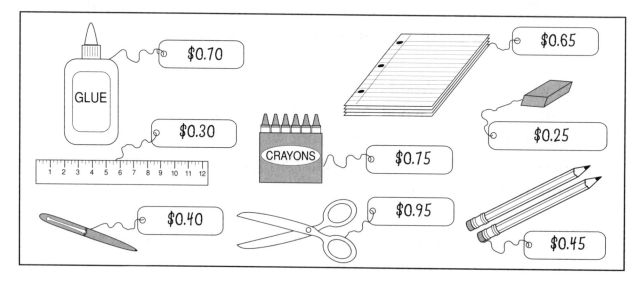

Opportunity Cost

An opportunity is a chance to do something. Let's say someone invites you to a party. You have an opportunity to go to the party. You must choose if you want to go. Let's say someone else invites you to go to the mall. The trip to the mall is at the same time as the party. Now you have two opportunities to go somewhere. Which will you choose? Would you have more fun at the party or at the mall? What would you lose if you chose one instead of the other?

When you make a choice between two things, you lose the opportunity to do one of them. That loss is called your **opportunity cost**.

Often, consumers have many choices in the market. They may find bread by several different bakers. They may choose between cars sold by different car dealers. They may buy one kind of shoe instead of another kind. Consumers must decide what they will gain or lose by their choices. They must consider their opportunity costs.

Directions Write complete sentences to answer the questions.

1. You want a new cap. The cap you want costs $5.00 at Hat Hut. You have the opportunity to buy the same cap for $3.00 at Cap Shack, but only on Friday. You choose not to go to Cap Shack on Friday. You buy the cap at Hat Hut instead. What is your opportunity cost?

   _____

   _____

2. Pretend you could go to the mall with your best friend. You can also go to a party at your new friend's house. You can choose only one opportunity. Which would you choose? On another piece of paper, tell why. Tell what your opportunity cost would be.

Name _____   Date _____

Chu's Shoes

Chu's Shoes makes and sells shoes. Four workers help in the production of the shoes. They divide the labor needed to produce each pair of shoes. One worker must buy the leather from another company. The second worker cuts out all the pieces. The third worker puts the pieces together to make a shoe. The fourth worker polishes each shoe. Working together, they can make more shoes in less time.

Another worker sells the shoes to consumers. Consumers like the products at Chu's Shoes. The shoes are well made. They have a good price, too.

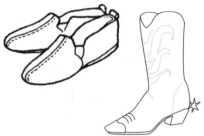

Directions **Write complete sentences to answer the questions.**

1. Is Chu's Shoes a producer or consumer?

_____

_____

2. Why do consumers like the products at Chu's Shoes?

_____

_____

3. Why is each worker important in the production of the shoes?

_____

_____

_____

Draw a picture of a shoe you might like to wear.

Name _____ Date _____

Making a Budget

Many people make a **budget**. They want to know how much money they earn. They need to know how much money they can spend to buy the things they want or need.

People earn money by working or by selling things. This earned money is called income. People must spend money to buy goods and services. This spent money is called expenses. If people have money left over, they often save it.

People must also pay taxes and fees to the government. In return, the people get goods and services from the government. Taxes and fees pay for these public goods and services.

Sometimes, people get goods and services without paying money. They trade instead of paying money to each other. This kind of trade is called barter.

Directions Look in newspaper ads and catalogs. What would you like to buy? Find out how much it costs. Then, complete the sentences. On another piece of paper, draw a picture of the thing you want to buy.

1. I want to buy _____.

2. It costs _____.

3. To get the money to buy it, I will _____

   _____.

4. To get the thing I want, I would be willing to trade my

   _____.

Income and Expenses

People can earn money in different ways. The money they earn is called **income**. People who have jobs earn money. Their income is known as wages. Teachers, doctors, and other workers all earn an income. A company can earn an income, too. Santee's Store sells food. All the money the store gets for selling food is income. Mario's Lawn Service mows lawns. People pay Mario for his service. A service company earns an income, too.

People cannot keep all their income. They must pay for the things they need or want. They spend money to get goods and services. The money they spend is known as **expenses**. Juwan earns an income by working. But he must pay for his house, his car, his food, and his clothes. Juwan has many expenses. A company has expenses, too. Santee's Store must pay for the food it sells. The store must also pay its workers. Santee's Store has many expenses, too.

Directions Complete the activity below.

Pretend that you can get any pet you want. But you must pay to buy your pet. You must also pay to take care of your pet. You do not have any money. On another piece of paper, write about your new pet. Which pet will you choose? What expenses will you have? What will you need to buy for your pet? What are the prices of these things? Tell how you will earn the money to buy the pet and supplies. How long will it take to earn the money you need? Will it take days, weeks, or months? Draw a picture of the pet you would like to get.

Name _____   Date _____

Taxes and Fees

People must pay **taxes** to the government. Taxes are collected to pay for schools and other goods and services. There are many kinds of taxes. If you buy something, you may have to pay sales tax. If you have a job, you may pay income tax. If you own a house, you have to pay a property tax.

The government also raises money by charging **fees** for certain goods and services. There are many kinds of fees. You must pay a fee to get your garbage collected. If you go to the park, you may have to pay a fee to use the swimming pool. You may have to pay a fee to park a car on a public street. If you ride the bus, you may have to pay a fee.

If people did not pay taxes and fees, the government would not have any money. Then, many of the goods and services would not be available.

Directions Each sentence tells something about the government and how it pays for services. Write **T** before each sentence that is true. Write **F** before each sentence that is false.

_____ **1.** Most people pay some kind of tax or fee to the government.

_____ **2.** A government gives the people all the services they want.

_____ **3.** Most government services cost money.

_____ **4.** Most money for government services comes from taxes and fees.

Public Goods and Services

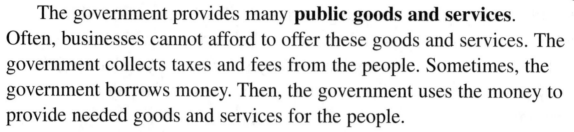

The government provides many **public goods and services**. Often, businesses cannot afford to offer these goods and services. The government collects taxes and fees from the people. Sometimes, the government borrows money. Then, the government uses the money to provide needed goods and services for the people.

The government provides goods such as roads, sidewalks, and bridges. Other public goods include parks, museums, and libraries. The government may also supply water and electricity for the people.

The government also provides service workers. Two important public services are police protection and garbage collection. The government also provides schools and health clinics for the people. The government may also have a public transportation system. The national government has an army to protect the people against other countries.

Directions Circle the goods and services that are paid for with tax money.

Savings

People may choose to save part of their income. First, they pay their expenses and taxes. If they have money left, they can save some for later use. The money they put aside is known as **savings**. They can open a savings account at a bank.

People save money for several reasons. Some people save money to buy something that costs a lot. For example, people save to buy a house or car. They save money to go to college. They may also save to pay for things they did not expect. Their house might need repairs. They might have sudden medical expenses. They can use their savings to pay for these unexpected costs.

Money in savings accounts makes more money. Savings earn income. This kind of income is called interest.

Directions You have just been given $100.00. How much will you spend? How much will you save? Write a short story. Tell what you will do with the money. On another sheet of paper, draw pictures of the things you might buy.

_____

_____

_____

_____

_____

_____

_____

Barter

Have you ever made a trade with a friend? You give your friend something. Your friend gives you something. You both get what you want, and you do not need to use money.

This kind of trading is called **barter**. Barter is trading without using money. People trade goods or services for other goods or services. People barter because they think they are getting a good deal.

Barter does not always work well. Each person must want what the other person has to trade. Both people must think that they are getting a good deal. They must believe that the trade is fair. If not, the trade will not happen.

Directions What is your favorite thing that you own? Pretend that your friend wants to trade you for it. Would you trade your favorite thing? What would you want in return? Write a story about two friends. Tell how they make a trade like this. On another sheet of paper, draw a picture to go with your story.

_____

_____

_____

_____

_____

_____

_____

_____

_____

Nick's Budget

Nick works for Chu's Shoes. He earns a good income working there. But he has many expenses. He must pay rent for his house. He must buy gasoline for his car. He needs food and clothes. He has to pay taxes and fees. He likes to go to the movies every weekend, too.

Nick makes birdhouses as a hobby. He sells them to earn extra money for savings. Sometimes, he makes a trade with Mario's Lawn Service. He gives Mario birdhouses to sell to his customers. In return, Mario cares for Nick's lawn. Both Nick and Mario like their barter.

Directions Write complete sentences to answer the questions.

1. How does Nick earn an income? _____

   _____

2. What are three of Nick's expenses? _____

   _____

   _____

3. How does Nick make extra money for savings?

   _____

   _____

4. What do Nick and Mario trade? _____

   _____

   _____

What Kind of Resource?

Production makes use of all the resources. The human resources are the workers. The workers use natural resources, or raw materials, to make a product. The workers also use capital resources, or equipment, to help them to make the product.

Directions The box has the names of different resources. List each name under the kind of resource it is.

hammer	fish
coal	judge
scientist	water
oil	desk
bus driver	copy machine
computer	trees
telephone	secretary
carpenter	

Natural Resources	Human Resources	Capital Resources
_____	_____	_____
_____	_____	_____
_____	_____	_____
_____	_____	_____
_____	_____	_____
_____	_____	_____

COUPON for Extra Credit

What other resources can you think of? Add another name to each column.

Name _____   Date _____

Goods or Resources?

Directions Look at the words in the box. Which are goods, and which are resources? Write each word in the correct list. Then, draw lines from the resources to the goods made from them.

oil	wheat
cotton	tomatoes
peanut butter	peanuts
trees	bread
tomato soup	shirts
gasoline	pencils

Resources	Goods

What other goods and resources can you think of? Write another resource in the first column. Then, write a good made from it in the second column.

From Trees to Boards

Directions Study the flow chart. Then, write complete sentences to answer the questions.

(Pick out a tree to cut down.)
(Cut the tree with a saw.)
(Trim small branches off the tree to make it a log.)
(Fasten the log to a tractor.)
(Pull the log to the loading area.)
(Place the log on a truck.)
(Drive the truck to the sawmill and unload the log.)
(Wash the log to remove the bark.)
(Saw the log into boards.)
(Stack the boards to dry.)

1. What is the first step in turning a tree into boards?

_____

_____

2. Which comes first, putting the log on a truck or pulling the log to the loading area?

_____

_____

3. What must be done after the log has been sawed into boards?

_____

_____

COUPON for Extra Credit

Draw a picture of one of the steps in the flow chart.

A Shopping Trip

Directions Draw a picture of what you would buy in each store. Then, draw a red circle around goods. Draw a blue circle around services.

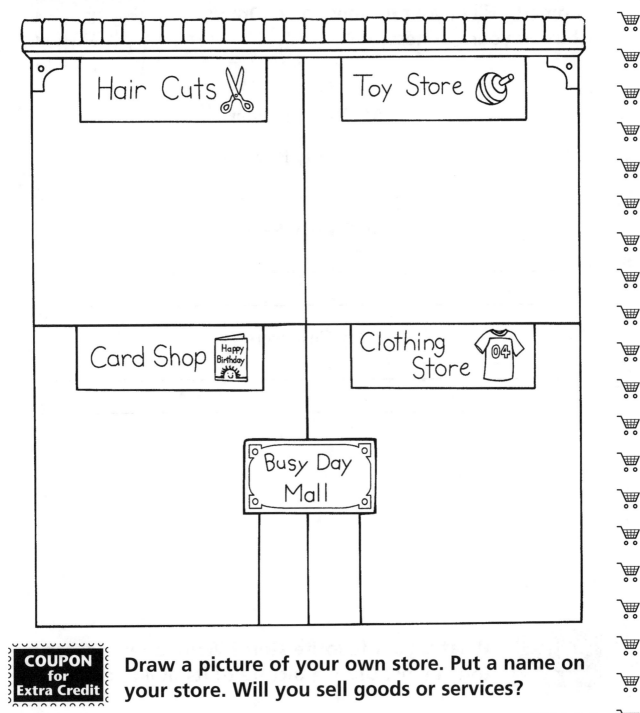

Hair Cuts

Toy Store

Card Shop Happy Birthday

Clothing Store 04

Busy Day Mall

COUPON for Extra Credit

Draw a picture of your own store. Put a name on your store. Will you sell goods or services?

A Business Plan

Directions Pretend that you are starting a
company. Give it a name. Will you make goods?
Will you provide services? Who will be your
customers? Fill in your business plan. Draw a
picture of your business.

My Business Plan

Name of My Business:

_____

My Good or Service:

_____

_____

My Customers:

_____

_____

COUPON for Extra Credit **What is your favorite store? Write a few sentences
to tell why. Draw a picture of its building.**

Shirt Production

Directions Complete the chart. Add words or pictures to show how a shirt is made.

1. _____
   _____
   _____

2. The cloth pieces are
   sewn together.

3. _____
   _____
   _____

4. _____
   _____
   _____

5. The shirt is
   put in a
   package.

COUPON for Extra Credit

Draw and color a picture of a shirt that you would like to wear.

Name _____   Date _____

Let's Build a Playhouse

Directions Complete the activity below.

Pretend that you want to build a playhouse. Three friends have agreed to help you. Look at the things below. You will use these things to build your playhouse. How can you divide the labor to make building the playhouse easier? What will each person do? Tell about your plan.

_____

_____

_____

_____

_____

_____

_____

Draw a picture of the playhouse you would like to build.

Name _____   Date _____

Snack Consumer

Directions You have $5.00 to buy snacks. Which two snacks will you choose to buy? How much change will you get back?

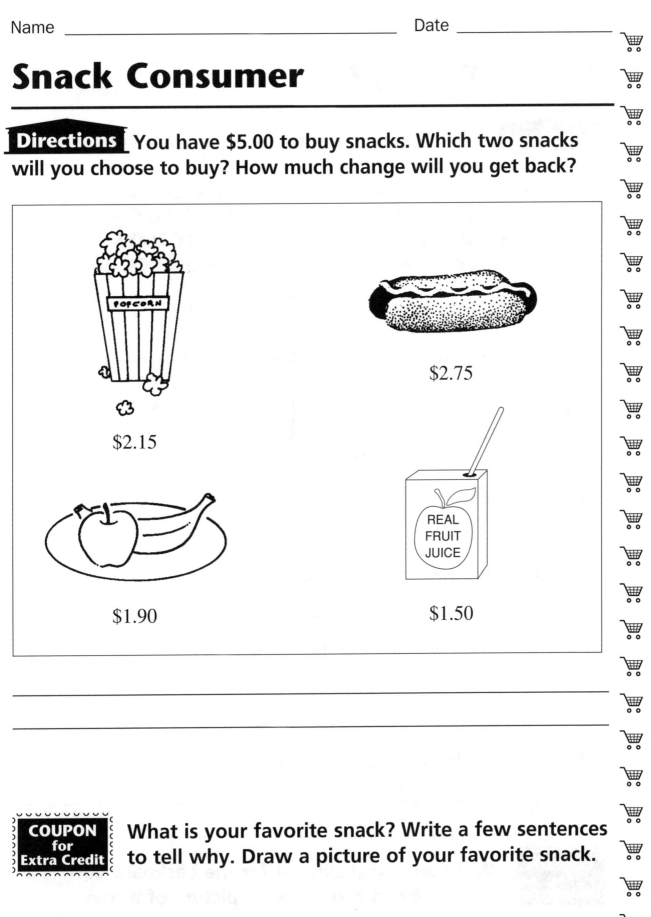

$2.75

$2.15

$1.90

$1.50

_____

_____

COUPON for Extra Credit What is your favorite snack? Write a few sentences to tell why. Draw a picture of your favorite snack.

Which To Buy?

Directions Read and compare the two advertisements. Then, answer the questions.

September Special **CARRY-ALL BACKPACK**	Back-to-School Sale **SUNNY DAYS BACKPACK**
• Sturdy, adjustable straps • Heavy-duty zippers • Waterproof material • Holds up to 40 pounds Red, Blue, or Green **Only $19.95**	• Popular Designs! • 3 Extra Pockets! • Comes in 6 Exciting Colors! **Yours for $17.95**

1. Which backpack costs less? _____

   _____

2. Which advertisement gives more information? _____

   _____

3. Which backpack would you choose, and why? _____

   _____

   _____

4. What would be your opportunity cost?

   _____

   _____

COUPON for Extra Credit

Write an advertisement for the backpack you would like to own. Draw a picture of it, too.

A Gift for Yourself

Directions What would you like to buy for yourself? Find out how much it costs. Make a plan to earn the money to buy it. What jobs can you do? How much money will the jobs pay? How long will you have to work? Write your plan below.

I want _____.

Its price is _____.

My income plan is _____

_____

_____

_____

_____

_____

_____

_____

_____

_____.

COUPON for Extra Credit Draw a picture of the gift you would like to buy for yourself.

Name _____   Date _____

Our Taxes Pay for Services

Directions In each box, draw a picture of a person doing a community service, such as fighting fires, delivering mail, or picking up litter.

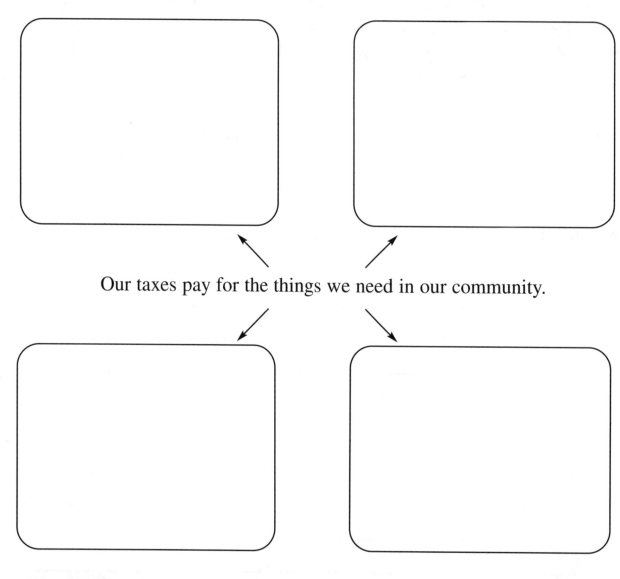

Our taxes pay for the things we need in our community.

COUPON for Extra Credit

Would you like to work for the government? What job would you like to do? Write a few sentences to tell why. Draw a picture of you doing that job.

Saving Your Money

Directions Think of something you would like to buy that costs $20.00. Pretend that you earn $5.00 a week for doing chores. Think of other ways to earn money. Make a plan. Write how long it will take you to save the money you need.

Goal: To earn $20.00 to buy _____

Ways I can earn money: $5.00 a week for chores _____

_____

_____

Money Earned	Money Spent

How long it will take to save enough money: _____

_____

 **COUPON for Extra Credit** Draw a picture of you playing with the thing you would like to buy.

Let's Make a Deal!

What is a good deal? What is a fair trade? We can make a fair trade by comparing the prices of the goods or services. How much does one new pencil cost? How much do five new pencils cost? Is a trade of one pencil for five pencils fair? Usually not. But you must decide about the trade yourself. Do you have a good reason for the trade?

Directions Help Su Li and Eve make a trade. Su Li has three things he wants to trade. Eve also has three things. Choose one thing that Su Li has. Choose one thing that Eve has. Draw a line between the two things. Then, tell why you think they make a fair trade.

COUPON for Extra Credit

Draw pictures of two things that you think would make a fair trade. Write a few sentences to tell why the trade is fair.

Basics of Economics, Grade 3

Answer Key

Overall Pretest, pp. 3–4
1. B, **2.** C, **3.** A, **4.** B, **5.** A, **6.** B, **7.** C, **8.** C
9. Answers will vary, but students should probably choose the $4 baseball because its price is $1 less.
10. Answers will vary, but students should indicate three reasonable ways to get the extra money they need.

Overall Posttest, pp. 5–6
1. A, **2.** C, **3.** B, **4.** B, **5.** A, **6.** A, **7.** C, **8.** B
9. Answers will vary, but students should include such expenses as a cage, food, shavings, toys, and medical care.
10. Answers will vary, but students should probably point out that the trade is not a good one because the backpack is worth more than the old pens.

Vocabulary Pretest, pp. 7–8
1. B, **2.** A, **3.** B, **4.** B, **5.** C, **6.** A, **7.** A, **8.** B, **9.** C, **10.** B, **11.** A, **12.** B, **13.** A, **14.** B, **15.** C, **16.** A

Vocabulary Posttest, pp. 9–10
1. C, **2.** B, **3.** B, **4.** C, **5.** B, **6.** A, **7.** C, **8.** A, **9.** A, **10.** A, **11.** A, **12.** C, **13.** A, **14.** B, **15.** C, **16.** C

Applications Pretest, p. 11
Answers will vary but should include reasonable responses and reasons.

Applications Posttest, p. 12
Answers will vary but should include reasonable ingredients and appropriate classification.

p. 13
Answers will vary.

p. 14
Students should draw a circle around the tree, rain cloud, fish, and land. Students should draw a square around the ball, pencil, and house.

p. 15
Across:
1. cook, **2.** teacher, **3.** driver
Down:
1. clerk, **4.** farmer, **5.** actor, **6.** money

p. 16
Answers will vary but should include such answers as the school building, the chalkboard, chalk, erasers, computers, books, pencils, pens, paper, art supplies, etc.

p. 17
1. Answers will vary but should include reasonable responses, such as water or oil.
2. Answers will vary but should include reasonable responses, such as carpooling, recycling, etc.

p. 18
Answers may vary slightly.
Goods: baker, farmer;
Services: judge, dentist, police officer.

p. 19
1. Mario operates a lawn care service.
2. Mario uses gasoline, saws, shovels, and other tools. (Some students may include mowers, plants, dirt, and rocks.)
3. Mario uses the human resources of Michael, Teeka, and himself.
4. Mario uses lawn mowers as capital resources. (Some students may also include saws, shovels, and tools.)
5. Mario uses the natural resources of plants, dirt, and rocks.

p. 20
Answers will vary. Check students' lists and pictures.

p. 21
1. B, **2.** A, **3.** B, **4.** C

p. 22
1. services, **2.** buy, **3.** sell

p. 23
Answers will vary. Some students might suggest that the other workers could fill in for Earl, but point out that quality might suffer. Another worker with skills similar to Earl's could be hired temporarily. Or the owner could have the other workers continue making furniture and wait for Earl to return to finish it.

p. 24
Answers will vary. Check that each student's choices do not exceed the $3.00 limit.

p. 25
1. The opportunity cost is $2.
2. Answers will vary but should point out what might be lost by choosing one opportunity instead of the other.

p. 26
1. In this example, Chu's Shoes is both a producer and a consumer.
2. Consumers like the products at Chu's Shoes because they are well made and priced right.
3. Each worker has a special role in producing the finished product.

p. 27
Answers will vary. Check students' pictures.

Basics of Economics, Grade 3

Answer Key

p. 28
Answers will vary but should include reasonable estimates. Discuss with the students the various expenses associated with pet ownership, such as food, medical care, training, etc. Check students' pictures.

p. 29
1. T, 2. F, 3. T, 4. T

p. 30
Answers might vary. Students should circle the police officer, the teacher, the firefighter, and the library.

p. 31
Answers will vary but each student's calculations should not exceed $100. Check students' pictures.

p. 32
Answers will vary but should show evidence of a reasonable trade. Check students' pictures.

p. 33
1. Nick earns an income by working at Chu's Shoes. (Some students might also indicate he makes birdhouses for extra money, which would also be considered income.)
2. Answers will vary but should include three of Nick's expenses: house rent, gasoline for his car, food, clothes, taxes and fees, and movie tickets.
3. Nick makes birdhouses as a hobby and sells them.
4. Nick gives Mario birdhouses, and Mario cares for Nick's lawn.

p. 34
Answers may vary slightly.
Natural Resources: coal, oil, fish, water, trees.
Human Resources: scientist, bus driver, carpenter, judge, secretary.
Capital Resources: hammer, computer, telephone, desk, copy machine.

p. 35
Answers may vary slightly.
Resources: oil, cotton, trees, wheat, tomatoes, peanuts.
Goods: peanut butter, tomato soup, gasoline, pencils, bread, shirts.
Lines between these sets: oil, gasoline; cotton, shirts; trees, pencils; wheat, bread; tomatoes, tomato soup; peanuts, peanut butter.

p. 36
1. The first step is to pick out a tree to cut down.
2. Pulling the log to the loading area comes first.
3. The boards must be stacked to dry.

p. 37
Answers may vary slightly. Students should draw appropriate items for each store. Students should draw a blue circle around the Hair Cuts store and a red circle around the other three stores.

p. 38
Answers will vary but should include reasonable responses. Check students' pictures.

p. 39
Answers will vary but should include responses similar to the ones given here.
1. The cloth is cut out using a pattern.
2. Students should draw a picture of the cloth pieces being sewn together.
3. Buttons are sewed on.
4. The finished shirt is neatly folded.
5. Students should draw a picture of the shirt being placed in a package.

p. 40
Answers will vary but should include reasonable responses. Students may suggest that if each person does a separate job, the work will go faster.

p. 41
Answers will vary but students may choose no more than two items. Check to make sure they did not exceed the $5 limit and that they calculated correct change. You might ask the students why they chose as they did.

p. 42
1. The Sunny Days Backpack costs $2 less.
2. The advertisement for the Carry-All Backpack gives more information.
3. Answers will vary.
4. Answers will vary.

p. 43
Answers will vary but should include reasonable responses.

p. 44
Answers will vary. Check students' pictures. You might have a discussion about government workers who are paid with tax money.

p. 45
Answers will vary but should include reasonable responses.

p. 46
Answers will vary but should include reasonable responses. You might lead a discussion about which are the better trades. The trade between the three pencils and the box of crayons is probably the best trade.